D0459247

21st Century Skills Library

GLOBAL PRODUCTS

Toys

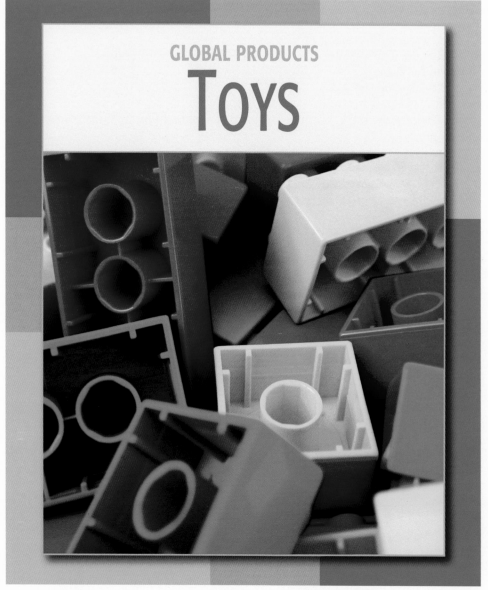

Kevin Cunningham

Cherry Lake Publishing

Ann Arbor, Michigan

Published in the United States of America by Cherry Lake Publishing
Ann Arbor, Michigan
www.cherrylakepublishing.com

Content Adviser: Michael Crawford, Toy and Collectibles Industry Consultant

Photo Credits: Cover and page 1, ©iStockphoto.com/ntr23; page 4, © Mira/Alamy;
page 6, ©Powered by Light RF/Alamy; page 8, ©iStockphoto.com/luminis; page
10, ©iStockphoto.com/VadimPO; page 13, ©Richard Sheppard/Alamy; page 15,
©iStockphoto.com/Sportstock; page 16, ©Darryl Webb/Alamy; page 19, ©iStockphoto.
com/alekcey; pages 20 and 26, ©vario images GmbH & Co.KG/Alamy; page 23, ©Opla,
used under license from Shutterstock, Inc.; page 24, ©Caro/Alamy

Map by XNR Productions Inc.

Library of Congress Cataloging-in-Publication Data
Cunningham, Kevin.
Toys / By Kevin Cunningham.
    p. cm.—(Global products)
ISBN-13: 978-1-60279-252-4
ISBN-10: 1-60279-252-6
1. Toys—Design and construction—History—Juvenile literature.
I. Title. II. Series.
TS2301.T7C75 2008
688.7'2—dc22   2008014186

*Cherry Lake Publishing would like to acknowledge the work of
The Partnership for 21st Century Skills.
Please visit www.21stcenturyskills.org for more information.*

TABLE OF CONTENTS

CHAPTER ONE

THE HISTORY OF TOYS

Store shelves are lined with all kinds of toys for kids to choose from.

Missy and her friend Carlos were sitting around Missy's room, trying to think of something to do. When Missy's grandfather walked in, he shook his head.

"It's a beautiful day," he said. "What are you doing?"

"We're bored," Carlos moaned.

"Bored? You have a roomful of toys."

"Grandpa Edgar," Missy said, "we've played with all these toys. We're tired of them."

Grandpa Edgar rubbed his chin. "Why don't you invent one of your own?"

"Nobody does that," Carlos said.

"People have been doing it for thousands of years," Grandpa Edgar said.

"No way," Missy said.

"It's true," Grandpa Edgar said, and he started to explain.

● ● ●

As long ago as 2200 BCE, children in parts of Pakistan pulled toy carts made of terra-cotta. A couple of thousand years later Chinese kids flew kites. In the Americas, the Naskapi people of Labrador made spinning tops out of wood. For centuries kids received handmade toys from relatives. Later, professional toy makers entered the picture. They created toys in workshops and sold them to people living nearby. By the late 1800s and early 1900s, companies were making toys in factories. Ignatz and Adolf Bing, brothers in Nuremberg, Germany, invented a line of toy trains that became so popular their company became the world's largest toy maker.

Learning & Innovation Skills

The toy industry is a huge business. That's especially true at holiday time, when corporations compete for attention and dollars. Mattel, Inc., of El Segundo, California, began in a garage making dollhouse furniture. Today, the Mattel empire covers four continents, employs 25,000 people, and leads the industry in total sales of its products. Henry and Helal Hassenfeld founded Hasbro, Mattel's main rival, in 1923. Hasbro's headquarters are in Pawtucket, Rhode Island.

In the last 25 years, the video game revolution has turned Nintendo, based in Kyoto, Japan, into a household name. Products such as the Game Boy DS and the Wii console have helped alter the way kids (and adults) play.

Toys have changed a lot since ancient times. What do you think the toys of tomorrow will be like?

Both children and adults collect Beanie Babies, a popular invention by Ty Warner.

In 1883, George S. Parker, a sixteen year-old Massachusetts **entrepreneur**, made $100 on a card game he invented and founded what came to be called Parker Brothers.

Margarete Steiff, part-owner of a German toy company, sewed together one of the first teddy bears in 1903.

In those days, toy makers built their products out of wood, metal (especially lead and tin), and cloth. Some started out as craftspeople such as carpenters or metalworkers. Their skills carried over into making toys. And their business sense, important for any entrepreneur, told them toys could make a profit.

The toy world changed again as the 20th century rolled on. Scientists in the United States and Europe had developed a family of new materials. Wood and tin toys were on the way out. The future belonged to plastic.

It may seem that the established toy companies are so powerful that a new entrepreneur doesn't stand a chance. Beanie Babies proved otherwise. Ty Warner got his start selling stuffed animals. After 18 years, he left the company he worked for and chose the life of an entrepreneur. He founded Ty Inc. and sold his first toys out of his condominium. Then he had a billion-dollar idea.

Warner designed nine "Beanie Babies." Drawing on his knowledge of what kids liked, he gave each a name and unique look. Using his knowledge of sales, he sold the toys in small shops to make them seem hard to find and special. To encourage kids to collect them, he kept the price low—about five dollars. He also produced new Beanies to replace the ones his company quit making. The original nine Beanie Babies hit the market in 1993. They soon exploded in popularity. In just six years, Ty Inc. was turning a bigger profit than Mattel and Hasbro.

The Westmont, Illinois, company continues to enjoy success. Meanwhile, Ty Warner, an entrepreneur with an idea, is worth between four and seven billion dollars.

CHAPTER TWO

MIRACLE MATERIAL

The foam inside the safety helmet that protects your head is usually made from a special type of plastic. The outside of the helmet is hard plastic.

"Plastic!" Carlos exclaimed. "My glasses are made of plastic. And my necklace. And the helmet I wore when I skateboarded over here."

"A lot of things are made of plastic," Grandpa Edgar said.

Missy held up a bucket she took to the beach. "But the plastic we wrap food in isn't like this plastic," she said.

"That's true," Grandpa Edgar replied. "We actually refer to a lot of substances as plastic, when they're not all the same. There's one kind of plastic called polystyrene. It helped make fast food possible because it's used for plastic forks and Styrofoam. The nylon and polyester in clothes are kinds of plastic. Lucite windows, Teflon cooking pans, the Kevlar body armor worn by soldiers, the Velcro on Carlos's shoes—plastic is behind them all."

"What makes them different, though?" Missy asked.

"A lot of it depends on how each is made," Grandpa Edgar said.

● ● ●

Plastic is what scientists call a **polymer**. Polymers are chains of molecules based in the element carbon, one of the most common substances on Earth. All living things contain carbon. In fact, the first polymers we learned to use came from plants. Rubber, a polymer harvested from trees in Africa and South America, became an important product in the early 1800s. Later in the century, the American inventor John Wesley Hyatt treated the plant polymer cellulose with chemicals and created celluloid. Manufacturers used Hyatt's versatile product in everything from dentures to ping pong balls.

A pumpjack is a machine that gets petroleum out of the ground. That petroleum can be used to make plastic.

In the early 1900s, scientists invented new polymers that didn't rely on plants. Using chemicals, heat, and pressure, new **synthetic** polymers were developed. A wide variety of plastics soon replaced natural materials such as wood, metal, cotton, silk, ivory, and bone.

Today's plastics use fossil fuels, and especially petroleum, as the main ingredient. Petroleum is a liquid or gas we extract from the ground. Major petroleum producers include Saudi Arabia (home of the world's largest petroleum field), Kuwait, and Venezuela.

People often connect petroleum with gasoline, one of its most important products. But in the United States alone, about 200,000 barrels of petroleum per day go to making plastic.

Untreated petroleum travels via ship or pipeline from an oil field to a refinery. There, intense heat and pressure separates the petroleum into a number of liquids, gases, and solids. Machinery pumps two of these substances, ethane and propane, into furnaces. A chemical **catalyst** is added to encourage molecules to bind together. The mixture becomes a powdery polymer called "fluff." Giant blenders mix the fluff with additional chemicals. These additives determine some of what a plastic can do. Additives can make it more fire resistant, or able to resist static electricity, or cause it to foam up. Colorants are one of the more common additives. As the name implies, colorants add color to the fluff. Once the additives are in, a machine melts the plastic. It then cools.

The next step is to run the raw plastic through the pelletizer. High-speed blades in the pelletizer cut it into pellets. Machine operators can set a pelletizer to make pellets in different sizes. A toy maker, for example,

Plastic made from petroleum creates chemical waste. Plastic products last decades or centuries as pollution. On top of that, petroleum is a **nonrenewable resource**. Once it's gone, it's gone. Cutting pollution and conserving petroleum mean finding alternative sources to go into plastic.

NatureWorks of Minnetonka, Minnesota owns a factory in Blair, Nebraska, where corn becomes plastic. The plastic comes from cornstarch. Manufacturers break the starch down into sugar, separate various elements, and then add chemicals to create a polymer called polylactic acid, or PLA.

Producing PLA takes an estimated 65% less energy and creates 68% less greenhouse gases. In addition, we don't need to worry about using up resources. Corn, unlike petroleum, is renewable. It can be grown every year.

might want pea-sized pellets, while another industry asks for pellets closer in size to grain.

For a plastic manufacturer, the pellet is the finished product. Tons of pellets go into shipping containers and are sent to factories. That's when the toy-making process begins.

CHAPTER THREE

BEHIND THE SCENES

*Many, but not all, toys are made with plastic. These
toy robots were made with thin sheets of metal.*

Missy held her drinking cup in one hand and a comb in the other. "So
the catalysts and additives determine the kind of plastic and what it can be
used for," she said.

"Exactly," Grandpa Edgar said. "Different toys require different kinds of plastic, too. No one wants a super-hard doll or a squishy fire truck."

"But you still haven't explained how people invent new toys," Carlos said.

"So now you're interested, eh?"

"Sure," Carlos said. "If I can make a billion dollars."

"It doesn't always work out that way," Grandpa Edgar said. "Sometimes individuals do come up with big ideas. But other times, it's the toy companies. And a lot of work goes into a new toy."

● ● ●

Toy companies have a special division called **product development** that's in charge of dreaming up new toys. Product development teams work for years on new products. Their ideas are kept secret.

Product developers start by doing research. They study past toys and what competitors are doing. They analyze how successful these toys were or weren't. They may also look at what competitors aren't doing. This process is often called brainstorming. Eventually, someone gets an idea. The team then looks into how much the new toy would cost, what supplies would go into it (and what the supplies cost), whether or not it would fit the company's image, and so on. If it needs special parts that cost too much, for example, the team drops the idea and moves on.

*In most companies, a group works together to
come up with new and exciting toys.*

It takes a lot of planning and many steps to create even simple-looking toys, like these Lego figures.

Many professionals have a say. One company developing a baby rattle asked for input from artists, engineers, toolmakers, and financial experts. They also got input from graphic designers who make packages for toys, buyers from large stores, child psychologists, and—of course—babies.

Once the team decides to go ahead, the company builds a **prototype**. The babies mentioned above played with a prototype of the rattle. Product developers then made changes to the toy based on how the babies played.

Approving a toy starts a whole new round of work. The factory may need new tools to make it. Designers must create packaging. Executives study financial information to determine how much to charge shoppers. All in all, it takes a huge number of decisions before factories order the plastic pellets for a new toy.

Where factories are located has changed a great deal in the past few decades. For many years, Lego manufactured its bricks at factories it owned. In 2006, however, the company decided to **outsource** a huge part of its manufacturing to a Singapore company called Flextronics, Inc. By choosing to outsource, Lego paid Flextronics to take charge of the company's industrial work. Lego employees could then focus on other tasks.

But Lego also outsourced its manufacturing to save money. Before, it had to pay high wages to workers at its home plant in Billund, Denmark, a plant in Switzerland, and at another plant in Enfield, Connecticut. The factories Flextronics owned, on the other hand, were located in Kladno, Czech Republic (a former Lego-owned plant); Sárvár, Hungary; and Juárez, Mexico. Workers in those places received far less money and fewer

21st Century Content

Toy companies can't always monitor what's being done in factories overseas. When things go wrong, outsourcing causes major problems.

RC2 Corporation, based in Oak Brook, Illinois, discovered that in June 2007. An RC2 plant in Dongguan, China, used lead paint on some of the company's most popular toys. Lead paint can cause brain damage and learning disabilities in children. The United States banned it from being used on toys in 1978. RC2 responded to the news by taking 1.5 million toys off the market.

Later that summer, Mattel found its own lead paint problem as well as design problems. By late 2007, more than 18 million toys made in China had been recalled. Though Mattel operates its own factories for popular toys like Barbie dolls, it outsources other work to about 50 Chinese companies. One of those firms had used the lead paint.

In September 2007, Chinese officials agreed to inspect toys and other products bound for the United States. This will help companies make sure that toys with lead paint stay off of store shelves.

benefits. The money saved became profit for Lego.

Outsourcing is a common business practice. Mattel and Hasbro have relied for years on Chinese factories, where workers make about $130 to $150 per month. Keeping prices down, and profits up, drives many of their competitors to do the same thing. Today, 70 to 80 percent of toys sold in the United States come from China. Not all manufacturing work goes to places like China, though. Corporations save money another way—by replacing human beings.

CHAPTER FOUR

THE TOY MAKER

Carlos hopped off the bed and grabbed a notebook. "Okay, so we're ready to invent a new toy and make it."

"You don't even know how to make toys," Missy said.

"Sure I do. We'll buy some plastic pieces and hammer them together."

"Making toys is far more complicated," Grandpa Edgar said. "Remember, Carlos, the plastic shows up at the factory

These plastic blocks are made from plastic pellets.

as millions of little pellets. First you have to shape them into what you want. Chances are, you won't need a hammer, either. In fact, machines, rather than people, do most of the toy making."

● ● ●

It's tough. It's hard. It lasts a long time. That's exactly what children and parents expect of the famous Lego brick.

*These green and yellow plastic pellets are
stored in silos at the Lego factory.*

Lego uses a durable plastic called acrylonitrile butadiene styrene, or
ABS. The ABS pellets arrive at a Lego factory by the ton in whatever colors
the company requires. Workers vacuum the pellets into a series of silos
for storage.

Lego, like all the large toy makers, uses an automated process to make toys. That is, machines do most of the work. Companies prefer **automation** for many reasons. Machines, for instance, make fewer mistakes than humans. They also cost less to use. Automation has taken over many kinds of industry in the United States, Japan, and Western Europe. It's a major reason fewer people work in manufacturing jobs today than in the past.

Toy production starts with the ABS pellets traveling through steel tubes. Their destination? An **injection molding** machine. Injection molding is a common process used for making plastic goods. The machine heats the pellets to about 450 degrees Fahrenheit (232 degrees Celsius). High pressure—between 24 and 150 tons of it—then forces (or injects) the melted ABS into a metal mold. Lego uses special steel molds treated with diamond dust and designed to precise measurements. Each costs tens of thousands of dollars. The mold shapes the ABS into a new Lego piece. Seven seconds later, the cooled piece drops onto a conveyor. Soon it tumbles into a hamper. The hamper shakes every few seconds. That way, the bricks settle without sticking together.

Every injection molding machine counts the pieces it makes. When a hamper is full, the machine makes a signal. A robot then carries the hamper to the next production stage. There, machines put together

the Lego toys built out of multiple pieces, like wheels, and stamp details such as faces or numbers onto pieces that need them.

Packing the Legos into boxes for sale is mostly automated, as well. A conveyor belt carries plastic (polypropylene) bags underneath a line of bins. Each bin contains different kinds of pieces. The bins release a preset number of pieces into each bag as it passes. The bag is then weighed. If it's even slightly off, a worker puts it aside. The people at the packaging table check a bag again before putting it into a cardboard box.

Throughout the process, technicians continually test pieces for quality and safety. Machines drop, pull, press, and bite down on pieces. This allows the technicians to make sure pieces won't break or otherwise become a choking hazard. Children can be rough on their toys. Toy companies have to keep that in mind.

CHAPTER FIVE

MOVEMENT OF GOODS

Containerships transport toys from one part of the world to another.

Missy looked over the toys scattered around her room. "A lot of these say 'Made in China,'" she said. "I get it. That means the companies outsourced the work to Chinese factories. But Mom bought some of these toys for me at the mall here in town, not in China."

"That's right," Grandpa Edgar said.

"But doesn't it cost a lot to send a doll from China to here?"

"Not compared to making it in the United States," Grandpa Edgar said. "Actually, the global economy today depends on shipping products cheaply across long distances."

Workers in China produce toys for a number of companies.
They are paid less than workers in many other countries.

It's the end of a work shift at a Mattel toy factory in Guanyao, China. Thousands of workers stream outside. Those with city apartments hop on their bicycles. But most head toward the company dormitories to rest after their eleven-hour workday. By China's standards, Mattel offers a good deal. Wages range from about $132 to $150 per month. The employees at the Guanyao plant also have access to medical facilities and cafeterias.

Changes in the global economy over the past 25 years have made it possible for China to grow into an economic powerhouse. One of the major changes has been the ways we transport goods.

Toys made in Guanyao are loaded into containers and carried by train, truck, or barge to port cities such as Shenzhen and Hong Kong. The containers are standardized, or all the same size—8 feet (2.4 meters) wide and about 8 feet tall. Only a container's length varies—it's either 20 feet (6.1 m) or 40 feet (12.2 m) long. Standardization allows shippers to store containers in the least amount of space. And every port, no matter where, can handle the cargo. If companies want profits, they have to ship containers of products as quickly and cheaply as possible.

Transporting toys from Mattel's factory to China's port cities is the first stage of the **supply chain**. The efficient movement of products along supply chains links the stores where we shop to faraway places like Guanyao. Once a load of containers arrives at a port, dockworkers use cranes, forklifts, and other heavy equipment to load them onto containerships.

Eight thousand of these massive vessels carry the load for the global economy. The largest of them would be the world's seventh-tallest building if you stood it on its end. A containership can make the trip from China to ports on the West Coast of the United States in about two weeks. When the

After toys are finished, they are sent to warehouses and then distributed to stores.

ship docks at its destination, workers on shore swing into action. This time the cranes and forklifts remove the containers. Each container comes with a list of its contents to make it easier to send the products inside to the next link in the supply chain.

Trucks and railroad cars carry loads of toys away. Some go to storage centers owned by the toy maker. Some go to **wholesalers** who sell discounted products. Still more go to warehouses and distribution centers owned by large store chains such as Wal-Mart and Target. The warehouses send the toys on to local stores.

It's a long way from China to U.S. stores. But the low wages paid to Chinese workers and the efficiency of global transportation make it cheaper to build a toy in Guanyao than in the United States

● ● ●

When Missy and Carlos returned to playing with the toys, both paused here and there to look them over, to check the labels and to remember Grandpa Edgar's story. Many parts of the world had touched each toy. Saudi oil workers may have extracted the petroleum for the plastic. Machines in the Czech Republic and human workers in Guanyao, China, had turned plastic pellets into toys. Dockworkers from Hong Kong to Seattle, truck drivers and train engineers across the United States, employees at distribution centers dotting the country—all played a part in getting toys into Missy's and Carlos's hands. Toys might be one of our oldest inventions. But they are also a modern product made possible by the new global economy.

21st Century Content

Guanyao is located in Guangdong Province. The hundreds of thousands of factories crowded into Guangdong make up the busiest manufacturing area in the world. Just nine cities make a significant share of the toys, cell phones, and footwear sold worldwide.

China's government decided to open its country to outside companies in the 1980s. Many of the workers came to cities such as Guanyao from the countryside. The booming industries constantly needed more employees. Young people in rural areas took city jobs. Though the wages were low by American standards, the jobs paid better than any work they could find in their villages.

Guangdong's workers have recently demanded more money and better working conditions. Some returned to their villages. Others traveled to better-paying factories in the Shanghai region. Suddenly, Guangdong factories had trouble keeping their workers.

The same thing happened in the past. When wages got too high in Taiwan and Japan, companies outsourced to China instead. Now, as Chinese workers demand more money, outsourcing will slowly move to less expensive nations. Experts predict the next outsourcing booms may take place in India, Vietnam, and Cambodia.

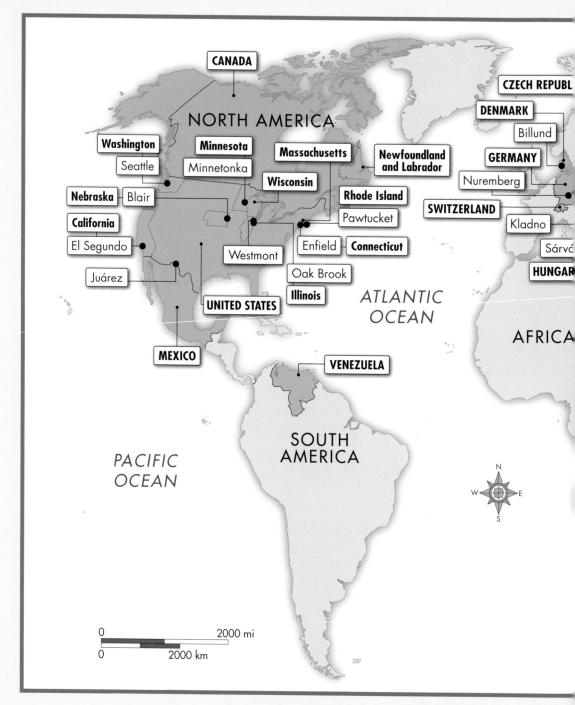

CANADA

NORTH AMERICA

CZECH REPUBL

DENMARK

Billund

Washington

Seattle

Minnesota

Minnetonka

Massachusetts

Newfoundland
and Labrador

GERMANY

Nuremberg

Wisconsin

Nebraska

Blair

Rhode Island

Pawtucket

SWITZERLAND

Kladno

California

El Segundo

Enfield

Connecticut

Sárvá

Juárez

Westmont

Oak Brook

HUNGAR

ATLANTIC
OCEAN

Illinois

UNITED STATES

AFRICA

MEXICO

VENEZUELA

SOUTH
AMERICA

PACIFIC
OCEAN

N
W E
S

0   2000 mi
0   2000 km

This map shows the countries and cities mentioned in the text.

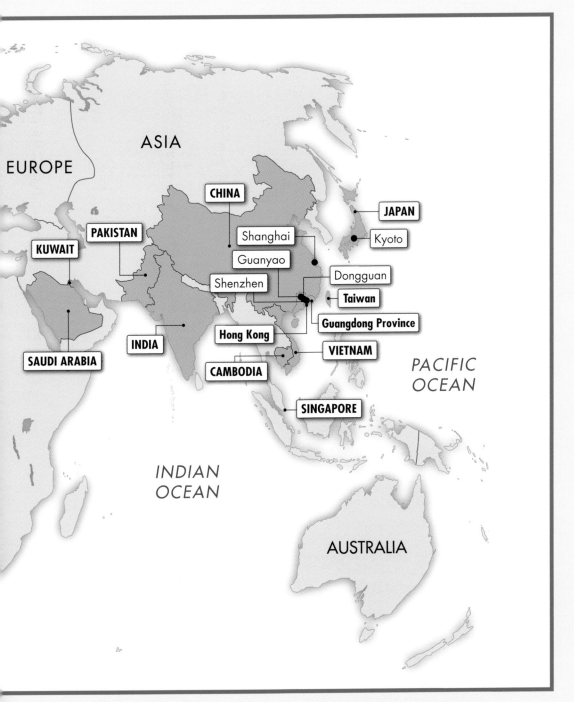

EUROPE

ASIA

CHINA

Shanghai

Guanyao

Shenzhen

PAKISTAN

KUWAIT

SAUDI ARABIA

INDIA

Hong Kong

CAMBODIA

SINGAPORE

Dongguan

Taiwan

Guangdong Province

VIETNAM

JAPAN

Kyoto

PACIFIC OCEAN

INDIAN OCEAN

AUSTRALIA

They are the locations of some of the companies involved in the making and selling of toys.

Glossary

automation (aw-tuh-MAY-shuhn) automation is a manufacturing process that uses (or mostly uses) machines in place of human workers

catalyst (KA-tuh-lust) a substance that starts a chemical reaction or makes a chemical reaction happen more quickly

entrepreneur (on-truh-pruh-NUR) an entrepreneur is a person who starts and then directs a new business

injection molding (in-JEKT-shuhn MOHL-ding) the injection molding process involves machines that melt plastic and then, using high pressure, inject it into metal molds in order to shape it

nonrenewable resource (non-ri-NOO-uh-buhl RI-sorss) a natural resource that cannot be replaced, such as petroleum, is considered a nonrenewable resource

outsource (OUT-sorss) for a company, to outsource means hiring an outside company to do manufacturing work

polymer (POL-uh-mur) a polymer is a substance formed by long chains of repeating molecules

product development (PROD-uhkt di-VEL-uhp-muhnt) companies organize product development departments to invent and perfect new products

prototype (PROH-tuh-tipe) a prototype is a working model of a new invention

supply chain (suh-PLYE CHAYN) a supply chain is a system of transport, workers, and other factors that connects raw materials to manufacturers and manufacturers to people who wish to buy a finished product

synthetic (sin-THET-ik) a synthetic substance is human-made or artificial

wholesalers (HOLE-sayl-urz) individuals or companies that buy a product in large amounts from a manufacturer and resell it

For More Information

Books

Finkelstein, Norman H. *Plastics.* New York: Benchmark Books, 2007.

Oxlade, Chris. *How We Use Plastic.* Chicago, IL: Raintree, 2005.

Web Sites

American Chemistry Council Learning Center
www.americanchemistry.com/s_plastics/sec_learning.asp?CID=1102&DID=4256
Learn how plastics are manufactured, used, and recycled

Hasbro Company History
www.hasbro.com/default.cfm?page=ci_history_hasbro
Information about the history of the Hasbro toy company

Mattel Company History
www.mattel.com/about_us/history/default.asp?f=true
Read about the history of Mattel toys

INDEX

ABOUT THE AUTHOR

Kevin Cunningham is the author of 30 books, including a series on diseases in history and a number of books in Cherry Lake's Global Products series. He lives near Chicago, Illinois.